Omelet Cookbook

An Omelet Cookbook Filled with 50 Delicious Omelet Recipes

By
BookSumo Press
All rights reserved

Published by
http://www.booksumo.com

Table of Contents

How to Make an Omelet 5

Beef & Bell Omelet 6

Mexican Steamed Omelet 7

Garden Omelet 8

Velveeta Omelet 9

Peas Omelet 10

Australian Shrimp Omelet 11

Mug Omelet 12

Georgia Omelet 13

Asparagus Omelet 14

Olives Omelet 15

Potato Omelet 16

Cheesy Bell Omelet 17

Simple Omelet 18

Japanese Omelet Treat 19

Two-Meat Omelet 20

Spinach Omelet 21

Fort Collins Omelet 22

Italian Cheese Omelet 23

Bell Pepper Combo Omelet 24

Mini Spinach Omelets 26

Creamy Olive Omelet 27

Italian Mushroom Omelet 28

Colorado Omelet 29

Japanese Omelet 30

Greek Olive Omelet 31

Japanese Rice Omelet 32

American Crab Omelet 33

Artichoke Heart Omelet 34

German Potato Omelet 35

Spanish Veggie Omelet 36

Indian Curry Omelet 37

Chinese Carrot Omelet 38

Yummy Mushroom Omelet 39

Sweet Apple Omelet 40

Eggplant & Tomato Omelet 41

Cheesy Bread Omelet 42

Double Cheese Omelet 43

Individual Bell Omelets 44

Yellow Squash Omelet 45

Cheddar Omelet 46

American Turkey Bacon Omelet 47

Super Healthy Omelet 48

Fluffy Cheese Omelet 49

Greek Feta Omelet 50

Mexican Sausage Omelet 52

The Classical Morning Omelet 53

Peas and Parmesan Omelet 54

Pesto Omelet 55

The Latin Omelet 56

How to Make an Omelet

Prep Time: 15 mins
Total Time: 55 mins

Servings per Recipe: 5
Calories	251 kcal
Fat	16.9 g
Carbohydrates	4.7 g
Protein	19.9 g
Cholesterol	332 mg
Sodium	591 mg

Ingredients

- 8 eggs
- 1 C. milk
- 1/2 tsp seasoning salt
- 3 oz. cooked turkey bacon, diced
- 1/2 C. shredded Cheddar cheese
- 1/2 C. shredded mozzarella cheese
- 1 tbsp dried minced onion

Directions

1. Set your oven to 350 degrees F before doing anything else and grease an 8x8-inch casserole dish.
2. In a bowl, add all the ingredients and beat till well combined.
3. Place the mixture into prepared casserole dish.
4. Cook in the oven for about 40-45 minutes.

BEEF
& Bell Omelet

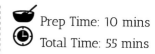
Prep Time: 10 mins
Total Time: 55 mins

Servings per Recipe: 2
Calories	511 kcal
Fat	29.5 g
Carbohydrates	26g
Protein	40.2 g
Cholesterol	105 mg
Sodium	284 mg

Ingredients

2 tbsp butter
1/2 green bell pepper, chopped
1/2 red bell pepper, chopped
1/2 Bermuda onion, sliced
7 baby portobello mushrooms, sliced

1/2 lb. beef tip
1/2 C. egg substitute

Directions

1. In a medium pan, melt butter on medium heat and cook mushrooms, bell peppers and onion for about 5 minutes.
2. Stir in beef and cook for about 5-10 minutes.
3. Stir in egg beaters and cook for about 10 minutes.

Mexican Steamed Omelet

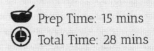

Prep Time: 15 mins
Total Time: 28 mins

Servings per Recipe: 1
Calories	484 kcal
Fat	33.7 g
Carbohydrates	7.9 g
Protein	37.7 g
Cholesterol	463 mg
Sodium	1322 mg

Ingredients

- 2 eggs
- 2 slices turkey bacon, chopped (optional)
- 1/2 C. shredded Cheddar cheese
- 1 tbsp chopped onion (optional)
- 1 tbsp chopped green bell pepper (optional)
- 2 tbsp chopped fresh tomato (optional)
- 1 tbsp chunky salsa (optional)
- 2 fresh mushrooms, sliced (optional)

Directions

1. In a large resealable freezer bag, crack the eggs.
2. Seal the bag tightly after squeezing out the excess air.
3. Carefully, squeeze the bag to beat the eggs.
4. Open the bag, and add the turkey bacon, cheese, salsa, mushrooms, green pepper, tomato and onion.
5. Seal the bag tightly after squeezing out the excess air.
6. In a large pan of the boiling water, add the bag and cook for about 13 minutes.
7. Remove the bag from the pan and carefully, open it.
8. Transfer the omelet onto a plate and serve.

GARDEN
Omelet

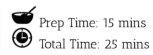
Prep Time: 15 mins
Total Time: 25 mins

Servings per Recipe: 2
Calories	739 kcal
Fat	48.8 g
Carbohydrates	6.4g
Protein	67.1 g
Cholesterol	532 mg
Sodium	4191 mg

Ingredients

3 tbsp olive oil
1/4 C. chopped onion
1/4 C. chopped green pepper
1 lb. turkey bacon steak, cut into small pieces
1 tsp garlic salt

5 large eggs
4 asparagus spears, chopped
2 tbsp milk (optional)
2 slices Provolone cheese

Directions

1. In a bowl, add eggs, milk and asparagus and beat till well combined. Keep aside.
2. In a pan, heat oil on medium heat and cook green pepper and onion for about 5 minutes.
3. Stir in turkey bacon and garlic salt and top with egg mixture evenly.
4. Add Provolone cheese slices and cook for about 3 minutes.
5. Gently fold the omelet in half and cook for about 2 minutes.

Velveeta Omelet

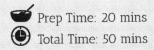

Prep Time: 20 mins
Total Time: 50 mins

Servings per Recipe: 6
Calories	266 kcal
Fat	12.5 g
Carbohydrates	21.2g
Protein	16.7 g
Cholesterol	216 mg
Sodium	749 mg

Ingredients

- 1 green bell pepper, chopped
- 1 onion, chopped
- 2 cloves garlic, minced
- 1/4 C. KRAFT Zesty Italian Dressing
- 1 lb. red potatoes, cooked, finely chopped
- 1 (6 oz.) package Smoked turkey bacon, chopped
- 6 eggs
- 1/2 C. milk
- 1/4 lb. VELVEETA, cut into 1/2-inch cubes
- 1/2 C. chopped fresh cilantro

Directions

1. Set your oven to 350 degrees F before doing anything else.
2. In a 10-inch oven proof skillet, add the dressing, onion, peppers and garlic on medium heat and cook for about 5 minutes, stirring frequently.
3. Add the potatoes and cook for about 5 minutes, stirring frequently.
4. Remove from the heat and spread the potato mixture in the bottom of skillet evenly.
5. In a bowl, add the eggs and milk and beat till well combined.
6. Place turkey bacon over potato mixture and top with the egg mixture, followed by the VELVEETA.
7. Cook in the oven for about 30 minutes.
8. Serve with a garnishing of the cilantro.

PEAS
Omelet

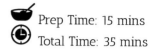

Prep Time: 15 mins
Total Time: 35 mins

Servings per Recipe: 6
Calories 165 kcal
Fat 7.4 g
Carbohydrates 17.5g
Protein 8.4 g
Cholesterol 104 mg
Sodium 104 mg

Ingredients

2 tbsp olive oil
1 small potato, peeled and diced
1 onion, chopped
2 cloves garlic, minced
1/4 lb. fresh crab meat, drained and flaked
salt and pepper to taste
1 small tomato, diced

1 (1.5 oz.) box raisins
1/4 C. peas
1 red bell pepper, chopped
3 eggs, beaten

Directions

1. In a skillet, heat the oil on medium heat and fry the potato for about 5-7 minutes.
2. With a slotted spoon, transfer the potatoes onto a aper towel lined plate and keep aside.
3. In the same skillet the onion and garlic on medium heat and cook for about 5 minutes.
4. Stir in the crab, salt and pepper and cook, covered for about 2 minutes.
5. Stir in the tomatoes and cook for about 2 minutes.
6. Stir in the raisins, bell pepper and peas and cook for about 2 minutes.
7. Place the beaten eggs over the mixture and cook for about 2-3 minutes.
8. Carefully, flip the omelet and cook for about 1 minute.
9. Serve hot.

Australian Shrimp Omelet

Prep Time: 15 mins
Total Time: 30 mins

Servings per Recipe: 4
Calories	292 kcal
Fat	20.1 g
Carbohydrates	7.6g
Protein	20.8 g
Cholesterol	292 mg
Sodium	306 mg

Ingredients

1 onion, diced
1 clove garlic, crushed
1/2 C. sliced fresh mushrooms
1/4 C. diced green bell pepper
12 medium shrimp - peeled and deveined
5 eggs
1/2 C. milk
1 tsp curry powder
salt and pepper to taste
1 tbsp olive oil
4 oz. shredded Cheddar cheese
1 tomato, sliced

Directions

1. In a medium nonstick pan, add the mushrooms, pepper, onion and garlic on medium heat and cook for about 5 minutes.
2. Stir in shrimp and cook till opaque.
3. Remove from the heat and keep aside.
4. In a bowl, add the milk, eggs, curry powder, salt and black pepper and beat till well combined.
5. In a skillet, heat the oil on medium heat and cook the egg mixture for about 5 minutes.
6. Place Cheddar cheese over the omelet, followed by the shrimp mixture.
7. Fold eggs over the filling and serve warm.

MUG Omelet

Prep Time: 15 mins
Total Time: 17 mins

Servings per Recipe: 1
Calories   217 kcal
Fat   13.9 g
Carbohydrates   1.5g
Protein   < 20.9 g
Cholesterol   213 mg
Sodium   503 mg

Ingredients

1 large egg
2 egg whites
2 tbsp shredded Cheddar cheese
2 tbsp diced fully cooked turkey bacon
1 tbsp diced green bell pepper
salt and ground black pepper to taste
cooking spray

Directions

1. Grease a microwave-safe mug with the cooking spray.
2. In prepared mug, mix together the egg, egg whites, turkey bacon, cheese, bell pepper, salt and ground pepper and microwave on High for about 1 minute.
3. Stir well and microwave on High for about 1-1 1/2 minutes.

Georgia Omelet

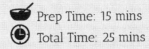

Prep Time: 15 mins
Total Time: 25 mins

Servings per Recipe: 3	
Calories	345 kcal
Fat	26.8 g
Carbohydrates	8.9 g
Protein	17 g
Cholesterol	397 mg
Sodium	647 mg

Ingredients

- 1 C. peeled, sliced peaches
- 2 tbsp lemon juice
- 4 slices turkey bacon
- 2 tbsp water
- 6 eggs
- 1 tsp chopped fresh chives
- 1/4 tsp salt
- 1 tbsp white sugar
- 1/8 tsp ground black pepper
- 1 pinch paprika

Directions

1. In a bowl, mix together the peaches and lemon juice and keep aside.
2. Heat a large, deep skillet on medium-high heat and cook the bacon till browned completely.
3. Transfer the bacon onto a paper towel lined plate to drain and then crumble it.
4. Reserve 1 tbsp of the bacon grease in the skillet.
5. In a large bowl, add the water, crumbled bacon, eggs, chives, sugar, chives, salt and black pepper and mix till well combined.
6. Reheat the bacon grease on medium-high heat and cook the egg mixture till set slightly.
7. Arrange the peach slices over the egg mixture.
8. Reduce the heat to medium and cook, covered for about 1 minute.
9. Uncover and cook till set completely.
10. Sprinkle with the paprika and remove from the heat.
11. Keep aside to cool slightly before serving.

ASPARAGUS
Omelet

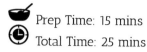 Prep Time: 15 mins
Total Time: 25 mins

Servings per Recipe: 1
Calories	537 kcal
Fat	39.2 g
Carbohydrates	11.2g
Protein	36.6 g
Cholesterol	421 mg
Sodium	938 mg

Ingredients

1 tbsp olive oil
2 eggs
1/4 C. milk (optional)
3 spears asparagus, trimmed and cut into 2-inch pieces
1/2 C. sliced fresh mushrooms
1/3 C. green onions, chopped
1/2 C. grated Parmesan cheese

Directions

1. In a bowl, add the milk and eggs and beat well. Keep aside.
2. In a large skillet, heat the oil on medium-high heat and cook the mushrooms, asparagus and green onions for about 4 minutes.
3. Place thee egg mixture over the asparagus mixture evenly and reduce the heat to medium.
4. During the cooking, carefully lift the edge to allow the uncooked egg to flow underneath.
5. When the omelet is almost done sprinkle with the Parmesan cheese and cook till cheese is melted slightly.
6. Carefully, fold in half and serve.

Olives
Omelet

🥣 Prep Time: 10 mins
🕐 Total Time: 55 mins

Servings per Recipe: 6
Calories	287 kcal
Fat	21.3 g
Carbohydrates	4.5g
Protein	20 g
Cholesterol	341 mg
Sodium	904 mg

Ingredients

10 eggs
1/3 C. milk
1/2 tsp salt
4 dashes hot pepper sauce
1/2 lb. turkey bacon - cooked, and chopped into bite-size pieces
1 (4 oz.) can black olives, drained
2 roma (plum) tomatoes, chopped
1/4 C. green onions, chopped
1/3 C. mushrooms, sliced
3/4 C. Colby-Monterey Jack cheese, shredded

Directions

1. Set your oven to 350 degrees F before doing anything else and grease an 8-inch square baking dish.
2. In a large bowl, add the milk, eggs, salt and hot pepper sauce and with an electric mixer, beat till frothy.
3. Add the bacon, mushrooms, olives, tomatoes, green onions and cheese and stir to combine.
4. Place the egg mixture into prepared baking dish evenly and cover with a piece of foil.
5. Cook in the oven for about 40-50 minutes.

POTATO
Omelet

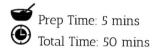

Prep Time: 5 mins
Total Time: 50 mins

Servings per Recipe: 7
Calories	247 kcal
Fat	18 g
Carbohydrates	10.2g
Protein	16.8 g
Cholesterol	243 mg
Sodium	534 mg

Ingredients

8 eggs
1 C. milk
2 C. shredded hash brown potatoes
1 C. diced cooked turkey bacon
1 C. shredded Cheddar cheese
salt and pepper to taste

Directions

1. Set your oven to 350 degrees F before doing anything else and grease an 8x8-inch square baking dish.
2. In a bowl, add the eggs and milk and beat well.
3. Stir in the turkey bacon, potatoes, cheese, salt and black pepper.
4. Cook in the oven for about 45-50 minutes.

Cheesy Bell Omelet

Prep Time: 20 mins
Total Time: 1 hr

Servings per Recipe: 2
Calories   386 kcal
Fat   29.8 g
Carbohydrates   9.1g
Protein   21.7 g
Cholesterol   430 mg
Sodium   1158 mg

Ingredients

- 2 tbsp butter
- 1 small onion, chopped
- 1 green bell pepper, chopped
- 4 eggs
- 2 tbsp milk
- 3/4 tsp salt
- 1/8 tsp freshly ground black pepper
- 2 oz. shredded Swiss cheese

Directions

1. In a medium skillet, melt 1 tbsp of the butter on medium heat and cook the onion and bell pepper for about 4-5 minutes, stirring occasionally.
2. In a bowl, add the milk, eggs, 1/2 tsp of the salt and pepper and beat till well combined.
3. In another bowl, place the cheese and keep aside.
4. Transfer the onion mixture into a bowl and sprinkle remaining 1/4 tsp of the salt.
5. In the same skillet, melt remaining 1 tbsp of the butter on medium heat and cook the egg mixture for about 2 minutes.
6. With a spatula, gently lift the edges of the omelet and cook for about 2-3 minutes.
7. Sprinkle the omelet with the cheese and then, place the onion mixture in the center of the omelet.
8. Gently, fold one edge of the omelet over the vegetables and cook for about 1-2 minutes.
9. transfer the omelet onto a plate.
10. Cut in half and serve.

SIMPLE Omelet

Prep Time: 10 mins
Total Time: 20 mins

Servings per Recipe: 4
Calories	128 kcal
Fat	0.1 g
Carbohydrates	0.8g
Protein	24.9 g
Cholesterol	0 mg
Sodium	371 mg

Ingredients

cooking spray
2 tbsp chopped onion
2 tbsp chopped green bell pepper
2 tbsp chopped mushrooms
salt and ground black pepper to taste
1 (32 oz.) container refrigerated pasteurized egg white substitute

Directions

1. Grease a 9x5-inch microwave-safe loaf pan with the cooking spray.
2. In the prepared loaf pan, mix together the bell pepper, mushrooms, onion, salt and black pepper. and top with the egg whites.
3. Microwave on High for about 3 minutes.
4. Remove from the microwave and stir the cooked egg white into the mushroom mixture.
5. Microwave on High for about 3 minutes.

Japanese Omelet Treat

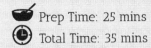

Prep Time: 25 mins
Total Time: 35 mins

Servings per Recipe: 1	
Calories	421 kcal
Fat	19.5 g
Carbohydrates	42.5g
Protein	20.9 g
Cholesterol	395 mg
Sodium	661 mg

Ingredients

- 1 1/2 tsp butter
- 1 small tomato, sliced
- 1/2 red bell pepper, sliced
- 1/4 onion, sliced
- 1/4 zucchini, sliced
- 1 oz. sliced mushrooms
- 1/2 C. warm cooked rice
- 1 tbsp ketchup
- 1 slice cooked turkey bacon, chopped
- 1/2 tsp paprika
- salt and ground black pepper to taste
- 2 eggs, lightly beaten

Directions

1. In a skillet, melt the butter on medium heat and cook the mushroom, zucchini, bell pepper, tomato and onion for about 5 minutes.
2. Stir in the bacon, rice, ketchup, paprika, salt and black pepper and transfer the mixture into serving plate.
3. Heat a nonstick skillet on medium heat and add the eggs in a thin layer.
4. Cook for about 5 minutes.
5. Serve the rice mixture with a topping of the omelet.

TWO-MEAT
Omelet

Prep Time: 15 mins
Total Time: 45 mins

Servings per Recipe: 4
Calories	539 kcal
Fat	38.6 g
Carbohydrates	4.3g
Protein	43.5 g
Cholesterol	645 mg
Sodium	852 mg

Ingredients

- 12 eggs, lightly beaten
- 3 slices cooked turkey bacon, chopped
- 3 slices cooked turkey meat, chopped
- 3 green onions, sliced
- 1 tomato, diced
- 1 sprig fresh parsley, chopped
- 1/2 medium green bell pepper, diced
- 1 (8 oz.) package shredded Cheddar cheese

Directions

1. In a bowl, beat 3 eggs well. Keep side.
2. Heat a lightly greased large skillet on medium heat.
3. Add the beaten eggs and swirl the pan to coat the bottom.
4. Cook, covered for about 2 minutes.
5. Top with 1/4 each of the chopped turkey bacon, turkey, green onions, tomato, parsley, bell pepper and Cheddar cheese and fold over the fillings.
6. Repeat with the remaining ingredients.
7. Serve warm.

Spinach Omelet

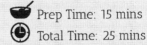

Prep Time: 15 mins
Total Time: 25 mins

Servings per Recipe: 2
Calories	363 kcal
Fat	26.9 g
Carbohydrates	6.3g
Protein	24.6 g
Cholesterol	425 mg
Sodium	839 mg

Ingredients

- 4 eggs
- 1 tbsp whole milk
- 4 pinches ground black pepper
- 2 pinches garlic salt
- 2 tsp olive oil
- 4 cremini mushrooms, sliced
- 2 tbsp chopped red onion
- 1 C. baby spinach, coarsely chopped
- 1/2 oz. crumbled Stilton cheese
- 1/2 C. shredded part-skim mozzarella cheese

Directions

1. In a bowl, add the milk, eggs, 4 pinches of the black pepper and 2 pinches of the garlic salt and beat well.
2. In a non-stick skillet, heat the oil on medium heat and cook the mushrooms and onion for about 5 minutes.
3. Spread the mushrooms and onion in the bottom of the skillet in an even layer and top with the spinach and egg mixture.
4. Cook for about 35 minutes.
5. Sprinkle the omelet with both cheeses and cook till cheese melts.
6. Fold the omelet in half and serve.

FORT COLLINS
Omelet

🥣 Prep Time: 15 mins
🕐 Total Time: 30 mins

Servings per Recipe: 2
Calories	402 kcal
Fat	29.2 g
Carbohydrates	7 g
Protein	28.7 g
Cholesterol	418 mg
Sodium	1212 mg

Ingredients

1 slice turkey bacon
3 eggs
1/4 C. milk
2 tsp vegetable oil
1/2 large tomato, diced
2 thin slices tomato, halved
5 oz. thinly sliced deli turkey
1/4 C. shredded Monterey Jack cheese
1/4 C. prepared hollandaise sauce
1 pinch dried parsley

Directions

1. Heat a large, deep skillet on medium-high heat and cook the bacon till browned completely.
2. Transfer the bacon onto a paper towel lined plate to drain and then crumble it.
3. Set the broiler of your oven and arrange oven rack about 6-inch from the heating element.
4. In a bowl, add the eggs and milk and beat till smooth.
5. In a skillet, heat the vegetable oil on medium heat.
6. Add the egg mixture and swirl the pan to coat the bottom of the skillet evenly.
7. Cook for about 1-2 minutes.
8. Gently flip the omelet over and cook for about 1 minute.
9. Transfer the omelet onto a broiler-safe baking sheet and top with the crumbled bacon, followed by the diced tomato, turkey and Monterey Jack cheese.
10. Fold the omelet in half to enclose the fillings and cook under the broiler for about 2 minutes.
11. Serve with a topping of the tomato slices, hollandaise sauce and parsley flakes.

Italian
Cheese Omelet

🥣 Prep Time: 10 mins
🕐 Total Time: 25 mins

Servings per Recipe: 1
Calories   598 kcal
Fat   41.7 g
Carbohydrates   10.9 g
Protein   44.1 g
Cholesterol   637 mg
Sodium   1215 mg

Ingredients

- 3 eggs, beaten until light and fluffy
- 2 oz. bulk Italian chicken sausage
- 1 tsp butter
- 1 pinch Italian seasoning
- 2 tbsp ricotta cheese
- 2 tbsp spaghetti sauce
- 2 oz. shredded mozzarella cheese

Directions

1. Heat a small skillet on medium-high heat and cook the sausage for about 4-6 minutes.
2. remove from the heat and discard the grease.
3. In a large skillet, melt the butter on medium heat and cook the eggs, sausage and Italian seasoning for about 4-6 minutes, lifting the edges occasionally.
4. Flip the omelet and top with the ricotta cheese and spaghetti sauce evenly.
5. Cook for about 3-5 minutes.
6. Sprinkle with the mozzarella cheese and fold in half.
7. Serve warm.

BELL PEPPER
Combo Omelet

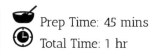 Prep Time: 45 mins
Total Time: 1 hr

Servings per Recipe: 2
Calories   419 kcal
Fat   24.5 g
Carbohydrates   12.6 g
Protein   20.4 g
Cholesterol   287 mg
Sodium   742 mg

Ingredients

- 4 slices peppered turkey bacon, cut into 1/2 inch pieces
- 2 tbsp minced garlic
- 2 tbsp minced onion
- 1/4 C. diced green bell pepper
- 1/4 C. diced red bell pepper
- 1/4 C. diced yellow bell pepper
- 1/4 C. diced orange bell pepper
- 1 tbsp chopped fresh basil
- 1 tbsp chopped fresh parsley
- 1 dash Worcestershire sauce
- 1 pinch cayenne pepper
- 1/4 C. vegetable broth
- 3 eggs
- 1 pinch Chinese five-spice powder
- 1/4 C. shredded Monterey Jack cheese
- 1/4 C. shredded Gouda cheese
- 1/4 C. salsa
- 2 tbsp sour cream
- 1 tbsp chopped fresh chives

Directions

1. Heat a large, nonstick skillet on medium-high heat and cook the turkey bacon for about 30 seconds.
2. Stir in the onion and garlic and cook for a few minutes.
3. Stir in the bell peppers, basil, parsley, Worcestershire sauce and cayenne pepper and cook for about 3 minutes.
4. Stir in the broth and simmer till all the liquid is absorbed.
5. Transfer the pepper mixture into a bowl and cover with a piece of the foil to keep warm.
6. In a bowl, add the eggs and five-spice powder and beat till smooth.
7. Return the skillet to the stove over medium-low heat and cook the egg mixture till just set.

8. Sprinkle with the both cheeses and cooking till the cheese begins to melt.
9. Place the pepper mixture over the omelet in a strip in the center.
10. Fold the sides of the omelet over the filling and transfer onto a plate.
11. Cut the omelet in half and serve with a topping of the salsa, sour cream and chives.

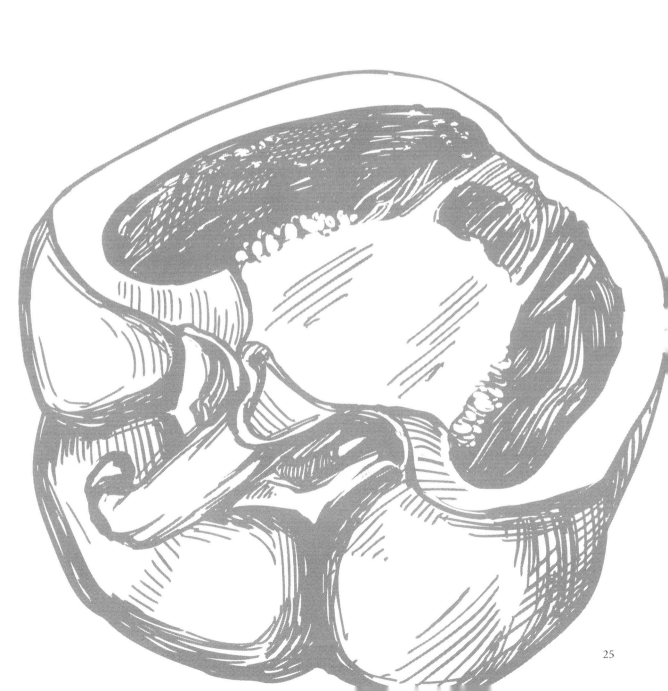

MINI
Spinach Omelets

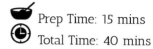

Prep Time: 15 mins
Total Time: 40 mins

Servings per Recipe: 12
Calories   123 kcal
Fat   8.2 g
Carbohydrates   2.1g
Protein   < 10.5 g
Cholesterol   22 mg
Sodium   223 mg

Ingredients

cooking spray
16 oz. egg substitute
1 (10 oz.) package frozen chopped spinach - thawed, drained, and squeezed dry
1 C. diced bell peppers

1 C. shredded Cheddar cheese
salt and ground black pepper to taste

Directions

1. Set your oven to 350 degrees F before doing anything else and grease 12 cups of a muffin pan with the cooking spray.
2. In a bowl, add all the ingredients and mix till well combined.
3. Transfer the mixture into the prepared muffin cups evenly.
4. Cook in the oven for about 25 minutes.

Creamy
Olive Omelet

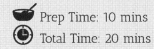
Prep Time: 10 mins
Total Time: 20 mins

Servings per Recipe: 2
Calories	627 kcal
Fat	46.6 g
Carbohydrates	10.8g
Protein	40.6 g
Cholesterol	419 mg
Sodium	740 mg

Ingredients

- 2 tsp vegetable oil
- 1/2 small onion, chopped
- 1 (5 oz.) can tuna, drained
- 1/3 C. sour cream
- 3 tbsp cream cheese
- 1/2 C. shredded mozzarella cheese
- 1 (2.25 oz.) can sliced black olives
- 1/8 tsp dried dill weed
- 1/8 tsp garlic powder
- 5 eggs
- 1/4 C. milk
- 2 tsp vegetable oil

Directions

1. In a large skillet, heat 2 tsp of the vegetable oil on medium heat and cook the onion till it begins to brown.
2. In a large bowl, mix together the tuna, cream cheese, sour cream, mozzarella cheese, olives, dill, garlic powder and cooked onion
3. In a large bowl, add the eggs and milk and beat well.
4. In the same skillet, heat 2 tsp of the oil and cook the egg mixture till set, lifting the edges occasionally.
5. Place the tuna mixture over one half of the omelet and fold the over the filling.
6. Cover the pan and remove from the heat.
7. Keep aside, covered pan till cheese is melted.

ITALIAN Mushroom Omelet

 Prep Time: 15 mins
Total Time: 25 mins

Servings per Recipe: 2
Calories 418 kcal
Fat 30.2 g
Carbohydrates 14.7g
Protein 21.6 g
Cholesterol 402 mg
Sodium 1292 mg

Ingredients

1/2 (14 oz.) can pizza sauce
1 (2 oz.) package sliced beef pepperoni
1/2 tomato, diced
1/4 C. diced onion
1/4 C. diced mushrooms
2 tbsp diced olives
1 pinch dried oregano
salt and ground black pepper to taste
1 tbsp olive oil
4 eggs, beaten

Directions

1. In a bowl, add the pizza sauce, pepperoni, olives, mushrooms, tomato, onion, oregano, salt, and pepper and mix well.
2. In a skillet, heat the oil on medium heat and cook the eggs for about 5 minutes.
3. Place the pizza sauce mixture over the omelet and cook for about 5-10 minutes.
4. Fold the omelet and serve.

Colorado Omelet

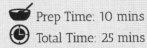
Prep Time: 10 mins
Total Time: 25 mins

Servings per Recipe: 4
Calories	367 kcal
Fat	20.1 g
Carbohydrates	30.5g
Protein	16.1 g
Cholesterol	219 mg
Sodium	627 mg

Ingredients

- 2 tbsp butter
- 1/2 C. sliced onion
- 1/4 C. chopped cooked turkey bacon
- 1/4 C. chopped green bell pepper
- 4 eggs, beaten
- 1/2 C. shredded Monterey Jack cheese
- 4 (8 inch) flour tortillas
- 1/4 C. salsa

Directions

1. In a skillet, melt the oil on medium-low heat and cook the turkey bacon, bell pepper and onion for about 5-10 minutes.
2. Stir in the egg mixture and cook for about 5 minutes.
3. Add the cheese and cook for about 2-3 minutes.
4. Divide omelet in tortillas and serve with a topping of the salsa.

JAPANESE
Omelet

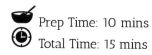

Prep Time: 10 mins
Total Time: 15 mins

Servings per Recipe: 1
Calories			82 kcal
Fat				5 g
Carbohydrates		2.9 g
Protein			6.6 g
Cholesterol		186 mg
Sodium			369 mg

Ingredients

1 tbsp water
1 tsp soy sauce
1/2 tsp white sugar

1 egg

Directions

1. In a bowl, add the sugar, soy sauce and water and mix till sugar is dissolved.
2. Add egg and beat till well combined.
3. Heat a nonstick skillet on medium heat and cook the egg mixture for about 3-5 minutes.
4. Flip and fold the omelet into a square and serve.

Greek Olive Omelet

Prep Time: 15 mins
Total Time: 23 mins

Servings per Recipe: 2
Calories   392 kcal
Fat   31.3 g
Carbohydrates   10.5g
Protein   19.1 g
Cholesterol   329 mg
Sodium   1014 mg

Ingredients

- 3 eggs
- 3/4 C. feta cheese
- 1/2 avocado, diced
- 1/2 C. diced tomatoes
- 1/4 C. chopped Kalamata olives
- 1 tbsp chopped fresh basil

Directions

1. In a bowl, add the eggs and beat till smooth.
2. Heat a nonstick skillet on medium heat.
3. Add the beaten eggs and sprinkle 1 side with the feta cheese, followed by the avocado, tomatoes, olives and basil and cook for about 5 minutes.
4. Fold over the omelet and cook for about 3 minutes.

JAPANESE
Rice Omelet

🍳 Prep Time: 5 mins
🕐 Total Time: 20 mins

Servings per Recipe: 1
Calories   521 kcal
Fat   20.2 g
Carbohydrates   59.3g
Protein   26.7 g
Cholesterol   403 mg
Sodium   1300 mg

Ingredients

1 C. cooked white rice
2 thin slices cooked turkey bacon, cubed
2 tbsp ketchup
1 slice processed cheese food (such as Velveeta) (optional)
2 eggs
salt and pepper to taste
1 tbsp ketchup
1/4 tsp chopped fresh parsley

Directions

1. Heat a greased skillet on medium heat and cook the rice, turkey turkey bacon, 2 tbsp of the ketchup and cheese for about 8 minutes.
2. Divide the mixture into a serving bowl and shape into an oval.
3. In a bowl, add the eggs, salt and pepper and beat well.
4. Heat a small greased skillet on medium heat and cook the egg mixture till set, lifting the edges occasionally.
5. With a spatula, gently fold the eggs into a cocoon shape and cook till set completely.
6. Remove from the heat and place the omelet on top of the rice.
7. Carefully, run a knife through the top layer of the omelet lengthwise.
8. Serve with a topping of the remaining ketchup and parsley.

American
Crab Omelet

Prep Time: 10 mins
Total Time: 22 mins

Servings per Recipe: 2
Calories	796 kcal
Fat	56.6 g
Carbohydrates	9.7g
Protein	61.6 g
Cholesterol	567 mg
Sodium	718 mg

Ingredients

- 2 tbsp butter
- 1/2 C. sliced fresh mushrooms
- 4 eggs, separated
- 2 tbsp milk
- 1 C. cooked crab meat
- 1 C. shredded Swiss cheese

Directions

1. In a large nonstick skillet, melt the butter on medium-high heat and cook the mushrooms for about 5 minutes.
2. Remove from the heat and with a slotted spoon, transfer the mushrooms into a plate.
3. In a small bowl, add the milk and egg yolks and beat well.
4. In another bowl, add the egg whites and with a dry beater, beat till soft peaks form.
5. Fold yolk mixture into whites.
6. Heat the same skillet on medium-high heat.
7. Place the egg mixture into skillet and top wit the mushrooms and crab meat evenly.
8. Cook for about 3 minutes.
9. Sprinkle with the Swiss cheese and fold omelet over, forming semicircle.
10. Now, cook, covered for about 3 minutes.

ARTICHOKE HEART
Omelet

Prep Time: 10 mins
Total Time: 26 mins

Servings per Recipe: 4
Calories   420 kcal
Fat   34.6 g
Carbohydrates   16.8g
Protein   10.9 g
Cholesterol   232 mg
Sodium   153 mg

Ingredients

16 frozen artichoke hearts, thawed
1/2 C. all-purpose flour
1/2 C. extra-virgin olive oil, divided
5 eggs

salt and freshly ground black pepper to taste

Directions

1. Sprinkle the artichoke hearts with the flour, shaking off any excess.
2. In a large skillet, heat 6 tbsp of the olive oil on high heat and cook the artichokes for about 8 minutes, stirring occasionally.
3. Transfer the artichokes onto a paper towel lined plate to drain.
4. Discard the oil.
5. In a bowl, add the eggs, salt and pepper and beat slightly.
6. In the same skillet, heat remaining 2 tbsp of the olive oil.
7. Add the artichokes and top with the eggs.
8. Cook for about 4-5 minutes.
9. Flip the omelet and cook for about 4 minutes.

German
Potato Omelet

Prep Time: 20 mins
Total Time: 35 mins

Servings per Recipe: 2
Calories	351 kcal
Fat	14.6 g
Carbohydrates	37.9 g
Protein	17.8 g
Cholesterol	266 mg
Sodium	440 mg

Ingredients

- 1 tsp butter
- 3 slices turkey bacon, cut into 1/2 inch pieces
- 2 potatoes
- 3 eggs
- salt and pepper to taste

Directions

1. In a large pan of the salted water, add the potatoes and bring to a boil.
2. Reduce the heat to medium-low and simmer for about 10-15 minutes.
3. Drain the potatoes and transfer into a large bowl to cool.
4. After cooling, cut the potatoes into 1/4-inch slices.
5. In a skillet, melt the butter on medium heat and cook the bacon strips for about 5-7 minutes.
6. Transfer the bacon onto a paper towel lined plate to drain and then crumble it.
7. In the same skillet, add the potatoes on medium-high heat and cook for about 5 minutes.
8. In a bowl, add the eggs, salt and pepper and beat well.
9. Place the cooked bacon and egg mixture into the skillet and stir to combine.
10. Cook for about 3-5 minutes, flipping once in the middle way.

SPANISH
Veggie Omelet

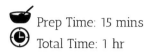
Prep Time: 15 mins
Total Time: 1 hr

Servings per Recipe: 6
Calories   252 kcal
Fat   21.5 g
Carbohydrates   10.7g
Protein   5.4 g
Cholesterol   124 mg
Sodium   54 mg

Ingredients

1/2 C. olive oil
1/2 lb. potatoes, thinly sliced
salt and pepper to taste
1 large onion, thinly sliced
4 eggs
salt and pepper to taste

2 tomatoes - peeled, seeded, and coarsely chopped
2 green onions, chopped

Directions

1. Sprinkle potatoes lightly with salt and pepper.
2. In a large skillet, heat the oil on medium-high heat and cook till golden brown and crisp.
3. Stir in the onions and cook till onion becomes tender, stirring occasionally.
4. Meanwhile, in a bowl, add the egg , salt and pepper and beat well.
5. Place the egg mixture into pan and gently, stir to combine.
6. Reduce heat to low and cook until eggs begin to brown on the bottom.
7. Carefully, flip the omelet and cook till set.
8. Serve with a garnishing of the tomato and green onion.

Indian Curry Omelet

Prep Time: 20 mins
Total Time: 30 mins

Servings per Recipe: 1
Calories	315 kcal
Fat	26.3 g
Carbohydrates	8g
Protein	11.9 g
Cholesterol	313 mg
Sodium	743 mg

Ingredients

- 1 tbsp light sesame oil
- 1/2 tsp minced garlic
- 2 tbsp minced onion
- 2 tbsp thinly sliced green onion
- 1/4 C. diced red bell pepper
- 1/4 tsp salt
- 1/2 tsp ground coriander
- 1/2 tsp ground cumin
- 1/2 tsp ground turmeric
- 2 eggs, beaten

Directions

1. In a skillet, heat the sesame oil on medium heat and sauté the garlic for about 20 seconds.
2. Stir in the bell pepper, onion, green onion and salt and sauté for 1-2 minutes
3. Sprinkle with the coriander, cumin, and turmeric and cook for about 30 seconds.
4. Spread the vegetables evenly over the bottom of the skillet. and top wish the egg.
5. Cook for about 30 seconds.
6. Roll the omelet and serve.

CHINESE
Carrot Omelet

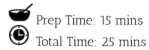 Prep Time: 15 mins
Total Time: 25 mins

Servings per Recipe: 4
Calories	131 kcal
Fat	8.6 g
Carbohydrates	6.1g
Protein	7.8 g
Cholesterol	186 mg
Sodium	82 mg

Ingredients

2 (3 oz.) packages enoki mushrooms, coarsely chopped
1/2 C. chopped green onions
1 small carrot, peeled and very finely chopped
4 eggs
2 pinches ground white pepper
1 tbsp vegetable oil

Directions

1. In a large bowl, mix together the eggs, carrot, mushrooms, green onion and white pepper and mix till well well combined.
2. With 2 tbsp of the egg mixture, mike each patty.
3. In a skillet, heat the vegetable oil on medium heat and add the patties in batches.
4. With the back of a spoon, press each patty lightly and cook for about 50 seconds.
5. Flip and cook for about 10-15 seconds.

Yummy Mushroom Omelet

Prep Time: 10 mins
Total Time: 25 mins

Servings per Recipe: 2
Calories	244 kcal
Fat	18.2 g
Carbohydrates	3.9 g
Protein	17 g
Cholesterol	376 mg
Sodium	352 mg

Ingredients

- 1 tbsp olive oil
- 4 large fresh mushrooms, sliced
- 1 tbsp chopped jalapeño pepper
- 1/4 tsp dried basil leaves
- 4 eggs, beaten
- 1/4 C. cottage cheese
- ground black pepper to taste

Directions

1. In a skillet, heat the oil on medium heat and sauté the mushrooms and peppers till soft.
2. Sprinkle with the basil and transfer into a bowl.
3. In the same skillet, add the eggs and cook till slightly done.
4. Flip the omelet and top with the mushroom mixture and cheese.
5. Sprinkle with the pepper and fold in half.
6. Cook till set completely.
7. Serve warm.

SWEET APPLE
Omelet

Prep Time: 20 mins
Total Time: 35 mins

Servings per Recipe: 4
Calories   148 kcal
Fat   3.6 g
Carbohydrates   25.7g
Protein   4.3 g
Cholesterol   106 mg
Sodium   164 mg

Ingredients

2 egg whites
3 tbsp white sugar
3 tbsp all-purpose flour
1/4 tsp baking powder
1 pinch salt
3 tbsp milk
2 egg yolks, beaten
1 tbsp lemon juice
1 tsp butter
1 large apple - peeled, cored and thinly sliced
1/4 tsp ground cinnamon
1 tbsp white sugar

Directions

1. Set your oven to 350 degrees F before doing anything else.
2. In a bowl, add the egg whites and with an electric mixer beat till foamy.
3. Add 3 tbsp of the sugar and beat till stiff peaks form.
4. In another bowl, mix together the flour, baking powder and salt.
5. Add the milk, egg yolks and lemon juice and mix till well combined.
6. With a rubber spatula, fold in the egg whites.
7. In a large oven proof skillet, melt the butter on medium heat.
8. Add the egg mixture and spread in an even layer.
9. Top with the apple slices and sprinkle with the cinnamon and remaining sugar.
10. Cook in the oven for about 10 minutes.
11. Cut into desired sized wedges and serve.

Eggplant & Tomato Omelet

Prep Time: 10 mins
Total Time: 1 hr

Servings per Recipe: 8
Calories	93 kcal
Fat	7.1 g
Carbohydrates	5.2g
Protein	3.3 g
Cholesterol	70 mg
Sodium	29 mg

Ingredients

- 1 large eggplant
- 3 tbsp olive oil
- 1 large tomato, diced
- 2 cloves garlic, peeled and minced
- 3 eggs
- salt and pepper to taste

Directions

1. Set your oven to 400 degrees F before doing anything else.
2. Wrap eggplant in a piece of the foil and cook in the oven for about 35 minutes.
3. Remove from the oven and keep aside to cool slightly.
4. Remove the skin of the eggplant and then, chop it.
5. In a medium skillet, heat the oil on medium heat and sauté the tomatoes and garlic till tender.
6. Stir in the eggplant and mash together with the tomato mixture.
7. Stir in the eggs and cook till set completely.
8. Season with the salt and pepper and serve.

CHEESY Bread Omelet

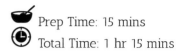
Prep Time: 15 mins
Total Time: 1 hr 15 mins

Servings per Recipe: 12
Calories 375 kcal
Fat 25.6 g
Carbohydrates 12.6 g
Protein 23.2 g
Cholesterol 193 mg
Sodium 692 mg

Ingredients

1/2 (1 lb.) loaf white bread, cut into cubes
1 1/2 lb. Cheddar cheese, shredded
1 C. cubed cooked turkey bacon
8 eggs
2 C. milk
1 pinch salt
1 dash hot pepper sauce
1/4 C. chopped green onion

Directions

1. Set your oven to 350 degrees F before doing anything else and lightly, grease a 13x9-inch baking dish.
2. In a large bowl, add the milk, eggs, green onions, hot sauce and salt and beat till well combined.
3. In the bottom of prepared baking dish, place half of the bread cubes and sprinkle with half of the turkey turkey bacon, followed by half of the cheese.
4. Repeat the layers once and top with the egg mixture.
5. Arrange the baking dish on top of a baking sheet with a rim.
6. Pour water into baking sheet and cook in the oven for about 60 minutes.

Double Cheese Omelet

Prep Time: 15 mins
Total Time: 25 mins

Servings per Recipe: 1
Calories	506 kcal
Fat	38.1 g
Carbohydrates	4.8g
Protein	34.9 g
Cholesterol	358 mg
Sodium	902 mg

Ingredients

- 2 eggs
- 1 1/2 tsp prepared horseradish
- 1 tsp salt-free herb seasoning blend
- 1/2 C. shredded Cheddar cheese
- 1/4 C. freshly grated Parmesan cheese

Directions

1. In a bowl, add the eggs and herb seasoning blend and beat till well combined.
2. Heat a lightly greased skillet on medium-high heat and cook the egg mixture till almost done.
3. Carefully, flip over and top with horseradish, Cheddar and Parmesan cheeses.
4. Cook till the bottom is set.
5. Fold in half and serve.

INDIVIDUAL Bell Omelets

Prep Time: 15 mins
Total Time: 35 mins

Servings per Recipe: 4
Calories   308 kcal
Fat   20.5 g
Carbohydrates   6.8g
Protein   23.8 g
Cholesterol   403 mg
Sodium   1008 mg

Ingredients

8 eggs
8 oz. cooked turkey bacon, crumbled
1 C. diced red bell pepper
1 C. diced onion
1/4 tsp salt
1/8 tsp ground black pepper
2 tbsp water

Directions

1. Set your oven to 350 degrees F before doing anything else and grease 8 cups of a muffin tin.
2. In a large bowl, beat the eggs.
3. Stir in the turkey bacon, onion, bell pepper, salt, black pepper and water.
4. Place the egg mixture into the prepared muffin cups evenly.
5. Cook in the oven for about 18-20 minutes.

Yellow Squash Omelet

 Prep Time: 10 mins
 Total Time: 25 mins

Servings per Recipe: 2
Calories	176 kcal
Fat	12.7 g
Carbohydrates	6.2g
Protein	10.2 g
Cholesterol	208 mg
Sodium	251 mg

Ingredients

- 1 yellow squash, ends trimmed
- 1 tbsp butter
- 1/4 C. fresh spinach
- 2 tbsp chopped fresh cilantro
- 2 eggs
- 1/4 C. milk
- 2 tbsp shredded mozzarella cheese
- salt and ground black pepper to taste

Directions

1. Through a spiralizer, make noodles from yellow squash.
2. In a skillet, melt the butter on medium heat and cook the squash noodles, spinach and cilantro for about 5-7 minutes.
3. Remove from the heat and spread the mixture in the bottom of the skillet evenly.
4. In a bowl, add the milk and eggs and beat till well combined.
5. Place the egg mixture over the squash mixture evenly and cook for about 5 minutes.
6. Sprinkle with the mozzarella cheese and cook for about 5 minutes.
7. Sprinkle with the salt and pepper and serve.

CHEDDAR
Omelet

Prep Time: 5 mins
Total Time: 25 mins

Servings per Recipe: 6
Calories 206 kcal
Fat 12.1 g
Carbohydrates 10.5g
Protein 13.4 g
Cholesterol 209 mg
Sodium 398 mg

Ingredients

6 eggs
1 C. milk
1/2 C. all-purpose flour
1/2 tsp salt
1/4 tsp ground black pepper
1 C. shredded Cheddar cheese

Directions

1. Set your oven to 450 degrees F before doing anything else and lightly, grease a 13x9-inch baking dish.
2. In a blender, add the milk, eggs, flour, salt and pepper and pulse till smooth.
3. Place the egg mixture into the prepared baking dish.
4. Cook in the oven for about 20 minutes.
5. Remove from the oven and sprinkle with the cheese.
6. Carefully loosen the edges of omelet and roll up omelet.
7. Transfer the omelet onto a serving plate.
8. Cut into 6 equal sized wedges and serve.

American Turkey bacon Omelet

Prep Time: 20 mins
Total Time: 12 hrs 20 mins

Servings per Recipe: 12
Calories   310 kcal
Fat   22.7 g
Carbohydrates   16.1g
Protein   19.9 g
Cholesterol   227 mg
Sodium   696 mg

Ingredients

1 (2 lb.) package frozen shredded hash brown potatoes
1 lb. diced cooked turkey turkey bacon
1 onion, diced
1 green bell pepper, seeded and diced
1 1/2 C. shredded Cheddar cheese
12 eggs
1 C. milk
salt and pepper to taste

Directions

1. Lightly grease a 4 quart slow cooker.
2. In a large bowl, add the milk, eggs, salt and pepper and beat till well combined. Keep aside.
3. In the bottom of the prepared slow cooker, place 1/3 of the hash brown potatoes in a layer and top with 1/3 of the turkey bacon, followed by the onion, green pepper and Cheddar cheese.
4. Repeat the layers twice and top with the egg mixture.
5. Set the slow cooker on Low and coo, covered for about 10-12 hours.

SUPER HEALTHY Omelet

Prep Time: 30 mins
Total Time: 30 mins

Servings per Recipe: 2
Calories	386 kcal
Fat	28.6 g
Carbohydrates	13.6 g
Protein	21.8 g
Cholesterol	358 mg
Sodium	561 mg

Ingredients

- 2 slices turkey bacon, chopped
- 1/2 lb. kale, stems removed, leaves cut into 1/2-inch wide strips
- 4 eggs
- 1 tbsp milk
- 1 tsp Dijon Mustard
- 2 tsp butter
- 1/2 C. Shredded Triple Cheddar Cheese with a TOUCH OF PHILADELPHIA
- 1/4 tsp ground black pepper

Directions

1. Heat a large, deep skillet on medium-high heat and cook the bacon till browned completely.
2. Transfer the bacon onto a paper towel lined plate to drain and then crumble it.
3. Reserve 1 tsp of the bacon grease in the skillet.
4. Place the skillet of the grease on medium heat and cook the kale for abut 5-6 minutes.
5. Transfer the kale into a bowl.
6. With paper towels, wipe the skillet.
7. In a bowl, add the milk, eggs and mustard and beat till well combined.
8. In the same skillet, melt the butter on medium heat and cook the egg mixture for about 5-6 minutes, lifting the edges occasionally.
9. Top with the cheese and cook till omelet is set.
10. Place the kale over half of the omelet and top with the bacon and pepper.
11. Slip spatula underneath omelet, tip skillet to loosen and gently fold omelet in half.
12. Transfer the omelet onto a plate.
13. Cut in half and serve.

Fluffy Cheese Omelet

Prep Time: 15 mins
Total Time: 37 mins

Servings per Recipe: 2
Calories   380 kcal
Fat   28.7 g
Carbohydrates   4.1g
Protein   26.2 g
Cholesterol   417 mg
Sodium   1030 mg

Ingredients

- 4 strips turkey bacon
- 1 tsp butter
- 1/2 sweet onion, diced
- 3 jumbo eggs
- 2 tbsp water
- 1/4 C. shredded sharp Cheddar cheese
- 1 slice process American cheese, diced
- 1/8 tsp salt
- 1/8 tsp crushed red pepper flakes

Directions

1. Heat a large, deep skillet on medium-high heat and cook the bacon till browned completely.
2. Transfer the bacon onto a paper towel lined plate to drain and then crumble it.
3. In another skillet, melt the butter on medium heat and cook the onion for about 10 minutes.
4. In a bowl, add the eggs and water and beat till well combined.
5. Place th egg mixture into a cold, greased 10-inch non-stick skillet.
6. Place the covered skillet on medium-low heat and cook till the steam starts to vent from the skillet.
7. Uncover and sprinkle with the crumbled bacon, followed by the Cheddar cheese, American cheese, salt, red pepper and onion evenly.
8. Gently, swirl the skillet in a circular motion to spread the omelet.
9. Transfer the omelet onto a plate and fold in half.
10. Keep aside for about 2 minutes before serving.

GREEK FETA
Omelet

Prep Time: 20 mins
Total Time: 30 mins

Servings per Recipe: 4
Calories   321 kcal
Fat   27 g
Carbohydrates   5.3g
Protein   15.5 g
Cholesterol   320 mg
Sodium   413 mg

Ingredients

2 tbsp olive oil
6 spears fresh asparagus, trimmed and chopped
1/2 red bell pepper, chopped
1/2 C. cherry tomatoes, halved
1/2 C. chopped fresh spinach
1/2 tsp minced garlic
1/2 tsp dried oregano
1/2 tsp dried basil
salt to taste
2 tbsp butter

6 large eggs
1/4 C. whole milk
1/2 C. crumbled feta cheese
1/4 C. shredded Cheddar cheese

Directions

1. In a large skillet, heat the oil medium heat and sauté the asparagus and bell pepper for about 3 minutes.
2. Stir in the spinach, cherry tomatoes, garlic, basil, oregano and salt and cook for about 3-5 minutes.
3. Remove from the heat and transfer the spinach mixture into a plate.
4. In a bowl, add the milk and beat till well combined.
5. In another skillet, melt the butter on medium heat.
6. Add the egg mixture and swirling the skillet to cover the bottom evenly.
7. With a spatula, pull up an edge of the omelet and tilt pan to run underneath.
8. Cook till the omelet is set, lifting omelet edge and tilting the pan occasionally.
9. Sprinkle with the salt.
10. Place the spinach mixture over one side of the omelet and sprinkle with the feta and Cheddar cheeses.

11. Gently fold half the omelet over the vegetables and cheese and press edges lightly to seal in the filling.
12. Cook for about 1-2 minutes.
13. Cut into desired sized slices and serve.

MEXICAN
Sausage Omelet

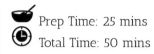

Prep Time: 25 mins
Total Time: 50 mins

Servings per Recipe: 8
Calories   307 kcal
Fat   19.8 g
Carbohydrates   15.8g
Protein   19.8 g
Cholesterol   137 mg
Sodium   827 mg

Ingredients

6 oz. beef sausage
1 small red onion, chopped
3 C. frozen Southern-style hash browns
1 (4 oz.) can chopped green chiles, undrained
1 (8 oz.) package Mexican Style Shredded Four Cheese with a Touch of PHILADELPHIA, divided

4 whole eggs
8 egg whites
1/2 C. Sour Cream
1/2 C. red salsa

Directions

1. Set your oven to 350 degrees F before doing anything else.
2. Heat a medium oven proof skillet on medium heat and cook the sausage and onions for about 8 minutes, stirring frequently.
3. Add the potatoes and chiles and cook for about 82 minutes, stirring occasionally.
4. Remove from the heat and stir in 1/2 C. of the cheese.
5. Spread the mixture in skillet in an even layer.
6. In a bowl, add the sour cream and eggs and beat till well combined.
7. Place the egg mixture over the sausage mixture and sprinkle with the remaining cheese.
8. Cook in the oven for about 25 minutes.
9. Serve with a topping of the salsa.

The Classical Morning Omelet

🥣 Prep Time: 10 mins
🕐 Total Time: 30 mins

Servings per Recipe: 6
Calories   630.1 kcal
Cholesterol   303.7mg
Sodium   1826.5mg
Carbohydrates   17.6g
Protein   27.9g

Ingredients

- 1 lb Jimmy Dean beef sausage
- 6 eggs
- 3 C. potatoes, chopped
- 1/4 C. onion
- 2 tbsps bell peppers, chopped
- 2 tbsps sweet red peppers, chopped
- 4 oz. monterey jack pepper cheese, chopped
- 4 oz. sharp cheddar cheese, shredded
- 2 tsps salt
- 2 tbsps half-and-half
- 2 tsps hot sauce
- 1/2 tsp baking soda
- 2 tsps pepper
- 2 tbsps olive oil

Directions

1. Set your oven to 350 degrees before doing anything else.
2. Fry your sausages then place them to the side.
3. Now fry your potatoes until they are brown, in oil, in a frying pan, then combine in the chopped pepper and onions.
4. Cook the mix until the onions are see-through.
5. Get a bowl and whisk your eggs then add in the baking soda, hot sauce, and half and half.
6. Add the eggs to the sausage mix in the pan then add your pepper jack cheese after dicing it then top everything with pepper and salt.
7. Top the mix further with the shredded cheddar and let the bottom of the frittata set in the pan.
8. Now place everything into the oven for 15 mins.
9. Enjoy.

PEAS and Parmesan Omelet

Prep Time: 15 mins
Total Time: 40 mins

Servings per Recipe: 4
Calories   199.7 kcal
Cholesterol   330.1mg
Sodium   206.2mg
Carbohydrates   9.5g
Protein   12.5g

Ingredients

- 6 eggs
- 1/2 C. evaporated low-fat milk
- 20 g butter
- 1 medium leek, thinly sliced
- 2/3 C. frozen peas
- 2 medium tomatoes, thinly sliced
- 2 tbsps finely shredded parmesan cheese
- salt
- pepper

Directions

1. Get a bowl combine evaporated milk and eggs.
2. Stir the mix until it is smooth then add in the pepper and salt.
3. Begin to stir fry your leeks in butter until they are soft.
4. Then turn on your broiler.
5. Add the tomato and peas to the pan then add the eggs.
6. Set the heat to low and let the bottom of the eggs set.
7. Once the bottom has set top everything with parmesan and place the frittata under the broiler and for 4 mins.
8. Enjoy.

Pesto Omelet

🥣 Prep Time: 10 mins
🕐 Total Time: 30 mins

Servings per Recipe: 4
Calories   384.1 kcal
Cholesterol   455.3mg
Sodium   322.0mg
Carbohydrates   22.0g
Protein   21.9g

Ingredients

1 tbsp oil
6 medium onions, sliced
1 tsp brown sugar
4 garlic cloves, chopped
8 eggs, beaten
3/4 C. milk
1/4 C. pesto sauce,
3/4 C. shredded cheddar cheese

salt, to taste
fresh ground black pepper, to taste

Directions

1. Get a bowl combine: pesto, milk, and eggs.
2. Begin to stir fry your onions after topping them with sugar, in oil, for 15 mins.
3. Combine in the garlic when 5 more mins of cooking time is left.
4. Now add in your eggs and let the bottom set for 7 mins.
5. Top the frittata with the cheese and some pepper and salt.
6. Now place the frittata under the broiler for 4 mins.
7. Enjoy.

THE LATIN
Omelet

Prep Time: 15 mins
Total Time: 40 mins

Servings per Recipe: 6
Calories   651.4 kcal
Cholesterol   441.2mg
Sodium   1439.4mg
Carbohydrates   17.1g
Protein   33.0g

Ingredients

- 1 tbsp olive oil
- 1 small onion, minced
- 3/4 lb beef sausage, chopped
- 6 oz. frozen tater tots, thawed
- 2 fresh garlic cloves, minced
- 1 C. roasted red pepper, chopped
- 12 large eggs, beaten
- 1 C. Monterey Jack cheese, shredded
- 1 large avocado, sliced
- 1/8 C. sour cream
- 1/8 C. salsa
- 3 tbsps scallions, finely sliced
- 3 sprigs cilantro leaves, for garnish

Directions

1. Add your tater tots to a bowl and mash them evenly.
2. Combine your sausage and onions in olive oil and stir fry them for 7 mins.
3. Then add in the tater tots, red pepper, and garlic.
4. Cook everything until the potatoes hot. Then add in the egg mix and combine everything evenly.
5. Set the heat to low and place a lid on the pan.
6. Cook the frittata until the bottom has set then place everything under the broiler for 3 mins.
7. Top the frittata with the cheese and let it sit in the pan with the lid placed on it.
8. Top everything with the cilantro, scallions, salsa, and avocado.
9. Enjoy.

Made in the USA
Las Vegas, NV
10 December 2023

82505847R00033